In nineteenth-century London with Dickens

In nineteenth-century
London
with Dickens

Text by Renzo Rossi
Illustrations by Alessandro Baldanzi

 **Marshall Cavendish**
Benchmark

New York

This edition first published in 2009 in North America by Marshall Cavendish Benchmark.

Marshall Cavendish Benchmark
99 White Plains Road
Tarrytown, NY 10591
www.marshallcavendish.us

Copyright © 2003 Italian edition, Andrea Dué s.r.l., Florence, Italy

Library of Congress Cataloging-in-Publication Data

Rossi, Renzo, 1940–
    In nineteenth-century London with Dickens / by Renzo Rossi.
        p. cm. — (Come see my city)
    ISBN 978-0-7614-4333-9
    1. City and town life—England—London—History—19th century—Juvenile literature. 2. London (England)—History—19th century—Juvenile literature. 3. London (England)—Social life and customs—19th century—Juvenile literature. I. Title.
    DA683.R77 2009
    942.1–dc22

                                                    2008033046

Text: Renzo Rossi
Translation: Erika Pauli
Illustrations: Alessandro Baldanzi

Photographs: p. 29, Scala Archives, Florence

Printed in Malaysia
1 3 5 6 4 2

Contents

Charles Dickens

Charles Dickens was born in Portsea, near Portsmouth, England, in 1812 to a modest family. His paternal grandparents were servants. His maternal grandfather embezzled funds and ran away to avoid arrest. Not even Charles's father, a clerk in the navy pay office, was without a blemish—he overstretched the family budget by spending more than he could afford, which landed him in **debtors' prison** in London in 1824. As a result, twelve-year-old Charles, like so many boys his age, had to leave school to work in a factory where he prepared shoe blacking. His hard and often unhappy childhood later surfaced in many of his novels, especially *David Copperfield*.

Dickens continued working even after his father was released from prison, and his schooling was therefore short and sporadic. He was proud, though, and was determined to show the world that he could be successful despite the misery and humiliation of his childhood. Dickens worked in a shop and as clerk to a lawyer before becoming a newspaper reporter for a parliamentary journal and collaborating on humorous publications. In 1833 he sent a story to the *Monthly Magazine*, the first in a long series collected into the book *Sketches by Boz*, published in 1836, which received favorable reviews from the critics. That same year he married Kate Hogarth, daughter of the editor in chief of the *Evening Chronicle*. He later left her and their ten children when, at the age of forty-six, he began an unfortunate and scandalous relationship with the young actress Ellen Turnan.

In 1836 Dickens also published his first novel, a collection of loosely related tales entitled *The Pickwick Papers*, which accelerated his writing career. The serial sold 400 copies at first, but sales rose to 40,000 when the story reached its climax in 1837. In this masterpiece of humor, Dickens created a myriad of characters from all social classes and presented an idealized and nostalgic picture of an England that was rapidly changing as the Victorian Age took hold.

Dickens's popularity grew with the novels that followed: *Oliver Twist* (1837–1838) and *Nicholas Nickleby* (1838–1839). The settings of both were characterized by the rise of industrialism, the consequent social problems, and the moralistic prejudices of the urban middle classes. Dickens mixed tragedy and comedy to paint the absurd and everyday life. Dickens first published his tale *The Old Curiosity Shop* (1840) in his weekly serial, but it was later printed as a book. In the wake of his success, Dickens gave lectures (upon payment) and organized and acted in theater performances.

In 1842 Dickens made his first trip to the United States hoping to find the principles of the French Revolution—liberty, brotherhood, and equality—embodied in the young democracy. His disillusion was expressed in *American Notes* and in the novel *Martin Chuzzlewit*, which sparked violent reactions in America. He published his most famous tale, *A Christmas Carol*, in 1843, after returning to England.

In 1846 Dickens returned to journalism. He founded the *Daily News*, which lasted only a year, and he directed the weekly *Household Words* from 1850 to 1859. He continued to publish novels and stories, which sold well but were more pessimistic and sharper in tone than his earlier works. These included *David Copperfield* (1849–1850), one of his most popular books and thought to be autobiographical; *Bleak House* (1852–1853), which advocates social reform; *Hard Times* (1854), an analysis of the industrial **proletariat** class; *A Tale of Two Cities* (1859), set during the French Revolution; and *Great Expectations* (1860–1861), a retrospective narrative about expectations in life. In the last phase of his life Dickens did not write much, but he gave highly successful public lectures and readings of his works. In June 1870 he suffered a stroke and died at Gad's Hill (Kent).

Though Dickens's novels were popular with the public, they received mixed reviews from literary critics. Some liked his unique characters and his social commentary, while others found his works to be overly sentimental with implausible plot twists. Although *The Pickwick Papers* is still considered a masterpiece of humor, his later novels have been criticized for excessive moralism. Nevertheless, Dickens was a literary giant during the Victorian Period and is considered one of the greatest nineteenth-century English authors.

Above: An illustration from a nineteenth-century edition of Dickens's novel *David Copperfield.*

Map of the City

London is a port city connected to the sea by the Thames River. The City of London first developed along the river and included some buildings famous today: the Tower of London, Westminster Abbey, and Parliament.

In 1666 London was almost completely destroyed by a fire. It was rebuilt with wide squares, spacious streets, and parks.

After the rebuilding, the residential quarters in Chelsea, Pimlico, and Bloomsbury became elegant and popular. Bloomsbury, in particular, was home to public administration buildings, museums, and universities.

The heart of old London, called the City and the Square Mile, is the business center. Square Mile is like a city within a city.

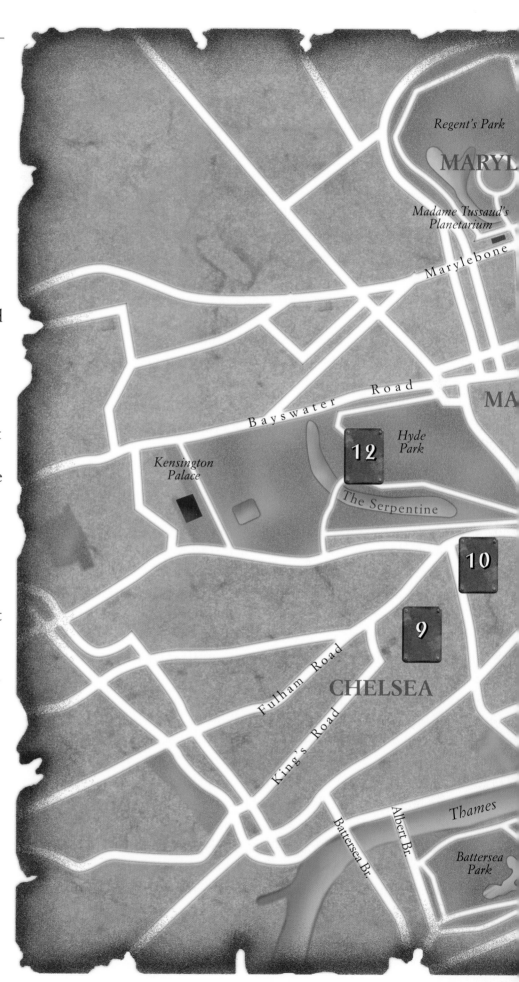

2

King's Cross
St Pancras

1

Dickens's
House

BLOOMSBURY

NE

Road

CITY OF
LONDON

3

Tower
of
London

St
Katherine's
Docks

IR

14

15

Strand

Waterloo Br.

Blackfriars
Br.

Southwark
Br.

London Br.

Tower Br.

4

13

Trafalgar
Square

Pall Mall

11

St James's
Park

6

Westminster Br.
Parliament
(Big Ben)

5

Buckingham
Palace

Westminster
Abbey

7

Lambeth Br.

PIMLICO

Vauxhall Br.

Vauxhall
Park

8

LONDON

Tower of London

Tower Bridge

St Paul's Cathedral
London Bridge

London!

Last month Mom and Dad celebrated their fifteenth wedding anniversary. Tomorrow my sister Alice will be 10 and last week I finished the 8th grade.

"Too many things to celebrate separately," Mom said. "Let's have one big present for everybody." So we decided on a trip to London, England.

You won't find me complaining! I love to travel and my parents are really cool. And, even though she's a girl, my sister Alice is good company. If you asked her she'd say the same thing about me: "Freddy's my brother, but he's pretty cool." As we admired the panoramic view of the city, Alice leafed through the guidebook and started pointing out things: "That's Saint Paul's Cathedral, with its great dome, and there in the background is Tower Bridge over the Thames. Right below is the City, the business center. The buildings that went up in the 1950s have already been replaced by ultra-modern glass-and-steel skyscrapers, but there are a few seventeenth- and eighteenth-century buildings, too. The Bank of England, entrusted with ensuring the monetary reserves of the country, has its headquarters in the City, but there are many private banks and institutes of credit and brokerage. It says here that the City, or Square Mile, should be visited during the week when the offices, which employ half a million people, are open. After five o'clock in the afternoon, there's no one around."

My sister likes to be the center of attention so I solemnly decreed, "In view of the competence she has displayed, the family assembly nominates Alice, here present, as official guide of this London sojourn." And, trying to keep a straight face, I continued, "You'll have to study a different itinerary every day and show us the most interesting places in London. You and I will draw them in our sketchbooks. As a reward you can have one ice cream a day, but only if you've earned it."

Alice laughed and accepted the challenge. But neither of us knew that the next day she and I would meet another, much more qualified guide—and even find ourselves in another London!

Dickens's House

The travel agency had reserved two rooms for us at the Oliver Twist Hotel, a small hotel in the Bloomsbury district. I was excited to see the Egyptian mummies and pharaohs at the nearby British Museum. Right around the corner was Doughty Street, a safe pedestrian area; Alice and I had permission to go out by ourselves to see what it was like walking around the London streets without a grown-up tagging along. We slowly wandered down Doughty Street, admiring the handsome brick houses with low wrought-iron railings.

"It's a nice hotel," said Alice. "I like the name too: Oliver Twist. Isn't that the title of a book we've got at home?"

"I believe you'll find it in almost all homes," said a deep, happy voice. "Actually *Oliver Twist* is a real best seller, although I shouldn't be the one to say so."

The speaker was a rather odd looking man in a long, old-fashioned, gray overcoat with a short cape and stiff high collar. He wore a top hat and carried a walking stick. I glanced at the gate he had just latched closed and noticed a sign: DICKENS'S HOUSE.

"Good day, my young friends. Have you come to visit my museum?" the man asked.

"What museum? And why do you say 'my museum'? Are you the owner?" I answered suspiciously.

"Quite a clever lad, aren't you," said the man not at all offended. "As you can see, this was the house of Charles Dickens, and I am none other than that gentleman to whom the museum is dedicated. So it's 'my' museum!"

"The writer?" I exclaimed, not believing my ears. "You're kidding! Charles Dickens has been dead for more than a 100 years—everybody know that."

"Great artists never die," replied the man. "When you read a book of mine, I am as alive as you see me now. And you, in turn, can enter and live in the world where my stories take place. What's so strange about that?"

"I believe you, sir. This is a cool game," said Alice, smiling like a Cheshire cat, a sign that she was up to something. And sure enough, suddenly she said, "Mr. Dickens, take us to visit the London of your novels. My name is Alice and this is my brother Freddy. We won't be any trouble! And I promise I'll read all your books."

"Fair enough," said Dickens, rather flattered. "If you see with your own eyes what London was like in the nineteenth century, you'll understand my *Oliver Twist* much better. Who would have thought a hotel would be named after him? Let's go. Keep close to me, Alice. And you, too, Freddy. Apparently you have decided I am not one of **Scrooge**'s ghosts."

Comings and Goings

Dickens told us our first stop would be an "exceptional" place. Alice and I were rather disappointed when we realized it was nothing but a railroad station, even if it was different from the ones we were accustomed to and looked sort of like a **Gothic** fortress. Well, I suppose a train station is a good place to start a trip.

"All aboard, ladies and gentlemen!" said our guide cheerfully. "This is St. Pancras Station. From here you can go to Liverpool and Manchester." He looked around and continued excitedly, "I adore this place. Doesn't it look like the chaotic gateway to adventure and the unknown?"

St. Pancras Station was covered by a glass roof on trussed iron arches that had a span of 243 feet (74 m). The largest glass roof in the world, Dickens pointed out with pride. Inside, the first thing we noted were the two enormous locomotives—one heading north, the other heading south—on either side of a wide platform packed with people and carriages. Trunks, bags, and other luggage were piled on the roof of the departing wagons and the travelers hurried to find their seats in the shaky coaches as if the train might suddenly lurch off.

"England has 4,500 miles (7,245 km) of railroad tracks," noted Dickens with great pride, "but some say there will be twice as many in ten years."

"Do you like to travel by train, Mr. Dickens?" asked Alice.

"To be honest, trains are a little modern for my taste. But, after all, times change. Right now, though, let's stop a cab: we have to go to all the way across town to the Tower of London. By Jove, I'll bet you children have no idea what fun it is to ride in a horse-drawn cab."

The Tower of London

3

"Don't let the name fool you. The Tower of London has at least twenty towers of all different shapes. They were built at different times, and each tower is two or three floors high."

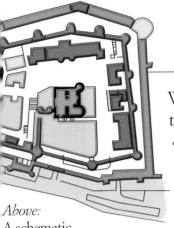

Above:
A schematic plan of the Tower of London. At the center (in green) is the White Tower, the original structure built by William the Conqueror in 1078. Buildings were added through the 16th century (red, violet, and ivory).

While Alice and I tried to draw what we saw in our sketchbooks, Dickens continued reciting facts, just like a tour guide.

"This grim monument, which has been standing for more than a thousand years, attracts millions of visitors. The Tower of London has served as a fortress, castle, state prison, and even death row for the aristocrats awaiting the executioner's ax."

It sounded like a rather boring lecture and I concentrated on my drawing until Dickens said, "…and so it will be, until the ravens abandon the Tower."

I looked up in surprise and saw that a raven had landed on his shoulder.

"What do you mean?" I asked.

"It's an old tradition. They say the British monarchy will fall as soon as these black birds leave for good."

"You don't have to worry, then," I reassured him. "The English monarchy is still secure. But tell me something about this white tower that we are drawing."

"That's the old **keep**. It stands on the remains of Roman walls built when London was called, as I'm sure you know, Londinium. There were storerooms and kitchens in the White Tower, as well as the apartments of the king and a cell for prisoners. Up there, in that round tower, is the tiny St. John's Chapel, one of the oldest churches in London. If you've finished sketching we can go and admire the crown jewels in the pavilion across the way."

Alice loves to try on our mother's jewelry, so she was excited to see what queens wore.

The Docks

When we left the Tower of London, our guide said we would visit the docks—the port district of London—which he called the lifeblood of the city.

"You know, Mr. Dickens, there aren't any more docks in my time."

"Stuff and nonsense, lad! Trade and industry would never survive without the docks, and London depends on those things to survive!"

"Maybe that's true in your time, but not in mine. The docks have been closed for years and years now. It's a fashionable residential area now."

"Closed, you say! Well, then I'll take you to St. Katharine Docks, which opened in 1828. You can't help but find them to your liking."

We went along a short stretch on the left

bank of the Thames. Most of the buildings were brick, to protect the goods from fire. It was a maze of shipyards, docks, warehouses, and industrial buildings.

"The industrial expansion," said Dickens, "brought people from all over England to the docks: engineers, carpenters, mechanics, blacksmiths, rope makers, and merchants. Skilled and unskilled laborers arrived with their families to work in the new shipyards, the new firms, and on the docks. It is a society in which the poorest, looking for work, live side by side with the well-to-do, looking for investments that will pay off."

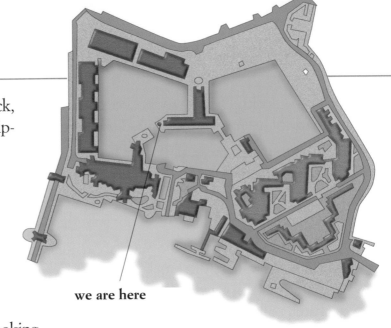

we are here

I had learned about the **Industrial Revolution** in school, but to see the people it affected directly was different. So many people lived in poverty because technological progress got rid of their jobs.

19

Hard Life in the Factory

After the docks, Dickens took Alice and me to an industrial suburb, where he had set so many of his novels. He wanted us to see how the working class really lived.

"This is the best time of day to get here: the short lunch break before the siren calls the workers back into the factory. Those women all work at the cotton factory," he continued. "They started work at dawn and don't leave until after sunset."

"The whole day?" asked Alice, not sure she had heard right.

"The hours are long, but the pay is more than they get as a domestic servant, although they don't earn nearly as much as the men. What makes it so hard is that it's like being in the army. You have to obey the rules and aren't allowed to stop. Supervisors and mechanical devices monitor the workers."

"They look as if they are already tired out," I said. "They'll have a hard time getting to the end of the day."

"This is progress, too," continued Dickens gloomily. "Once cotton was spun on a spinning wheel and woven into cloth at home on handlooms. Life was hard for women then, too, but at least they could have a vegetable garden or raise a pig or a couple of chickens to keep going when there was no work."

"And in the factory?" I asked.

"Once they're in the factory, the women have to obey the rules and regulations. They are dead tired when they get to bed. At eleven o'clock at night the workers' districts are so quiet they seem deserted."

Big Ben and the Palace

Westminster Palace, first the royal residence and then the parliament building, rose up across the river. Its honey-colored stone glowed in the sun.

"It looks new, Mr. Dickens," I said amazed. "I thought Westminster Palace was built centuries and centuries ago."

"Actually," answered Dickens, "the main part, Westminster Hall, was built around the middle of the eleventh century. It was enlarged and modified during the thirteenth and fifteenth centuries. It's one of the oldest buildings in the city, and one of the few that survived the fire in 1834."

"Did the fire destroy a lot?" I asked.

"If it weren't so serious, it might make me laugh." Dickens leaned more comfortably on a low wall overlooking the river. "Seventeen years ago some civil servant decided that the registers of the old state treasury should be organized and cleaned out. There were thousands of documents carefully rolled up in musty, moldy rooms. Some had been

The Parliament

Great Britain is a constitutional monarchy in which the monarch is the head of state and the prime minister, nominated by the sovereign, is the head of government. The king or queen represents the unity of the country and plays an important role in politics. There are two houses in the British Parliament: the House of Lords, which consists of appointed members, and the House of Commons, the members of which are elected by the public.

there for more than five hundred years. He decided that they should be burned. His men were careless and set fire to the whole building. By the next morning most of the palace was gone, except for Westminster Hall, the Jewel Tower, a crypt, and the cloisters."

"It must have been a spectacular sight," I said, impressed.

"People from all over London came to see the ruins, including me. Many were crying. You're looking at the reconstructed palace, which is even finer than the old one."

"I must say the style is rather unusual," I said admiringly.

"Look at all those spires and the clock tower called Big Ben. They were built in the medieval Gothic style," said Dickens.

"Why did they call it Big Ben, sir? It's an odd name," I asked.

"Officially, it was named in honor of Benjamin Hall, the prefect of public works. But if you ask around, everyone will tell you it's named after the boxer Benjamin Caunt—glory of national boxing, the man who never went down in the ring, as firm and indestructible as a tower—his nickname was Big Ben."

Westminster Abbey

A short walk from Parliament brought us to Westminster Abbey. The building towered over us and the great pointed window reflected the sunlight and almost blinded us. The two towers that rose up on either side looked as though they were squeezing the window.

"You can't build something like this in just one century. The abbey is the work of many people," said Mr. Dickens, "and every era has left its mark. The first abbey church was built by **Edward the Confessor** back in the middle of the eleventh century; he is buried here. Just two hundred years later **Henry III** commissioned a new building and hired great English and French architects. Work was interrupted more than once, but the essential parts of the church, including the nave, were finished around the middle of the sixteenth century. The towers, on the other hand, are relatively modern. They were built between 1735 and 1740. In fact, I'm not sure how workers built them that quickly."

"Your church is really beautiful," said Alice, "and anyone can see you're very proud of it."

"You're right, my lass," answered Dickens as we went inside. "Westminster Abbey is much more than a church. This is the shrine of British history. Kings are consecrated here on the oak chair. Fifteen of them are buried in the various chapels. But the abbey is also a great cemetery. Would you believe it? No less than five thousand tombs, sepulchral monuments, commemorative statues, and busts of those who served the country are housed in Westminster Abbey."

"All ministers, politicians, and military men, I imagine," I said a bit ironically.

"Not at all," he answered. "Intellects and artists also bring honor to their country. The head of the south **transept**, for example, houses the Poets' Corner. The greatest English poets and writers are buried or commemorated there. There are monuments to **Shakespeare**, **Byron**, and the German composer **Handel**, who chose England as his homeland. People like this are not just national glories; they are citizens of the world and what they have done belongs to all humanity."

"You're a famous writer, Mr. Dickens," I said, trying to make amends. "Do you know where your spot in this lovely abbey will be?"

"Of course I do!" he said laughing. "I'll do what Ben Jonson did."

"And who was Ben Jonson?" I asked.

"He was a playwright who lived during the sixteenth and seventeenth centuries—an exceptional figure in his time. He was hot-headed, but wrote vigorous works. He was determined to be buried in the abbey. 'I don't need much space, he would say, a square meter will do,' he said. So they buried him standing up!"

We were still laughing as we crossed back over the Thames and headed to Vauxhall Park.

Parks and Pleasures

"This," said Dickens, "is one of my favorite places and one of the main attractions of London. I sometimes come here with my friends to enjoy the fresh air."

We were on the right bank of the Thames, close to Westminster Bridge. It looked like a setting for a fairy tale: sweeping soft lawns, flower beds, artificial ponds and waterfalls, lush groves, pavilions, and hedge mazes. People were strolling, picnicking, riding horses, and resting in the shade.

"What a wonderful place," said Alice. "Honestly, Mr. Dickens, I can't complain about your choice this time."

"We're at Vauxhall Gardens," said our guide "one of London's pleasure gardens that make life in the city bearable. Everything here is meant to

please the eye and delight the spirit. Grottoes, Chinese pagodas, fake ruins. There is everything something for everyone. Nature couldn't have done a better job and we Londoners are mighty proud of it. There are others, like Cremorne in Chelsea, on the left bank of the river. But I like Vauxhall best and often come here in the evening."

"You come here at night?" asked Alice in surprise.

"Oh, evenings at Vauxhall are a dream. There are 20,000 gas lamps and Venetian lanterns. Every so often there are fireworks. People dance, eat, drink, and have a good time."

"And you call that getting a whiff of fresh air!" I said laughing. "You just like parties, Mr. Dickens, but I sort of suspected as much."

Horseracing

"Cool, Mr. Dickens, you've brought us to see the horses!"

When we left Vauxhall Gardens, our guide stopped a carriage and, after a short ride, we were in the suburb of Chelsea, across the river, where there was a hippodrome, or horse track.

"Forgive me, my dears," said Dickens, "this may not be Ascot or Epson, the most famous **turfs** in England, but Londoners can satisfy their passion for horses and betting here."

He led us to the central grassy area reserved for the public. As we walked along Dickens greeted a worker just coming off his shift just as politely as he did an elegant lady on the arm of a man in a top hat.

"No class distinctions on the turf," affirmed Mr. Dickens. "The great lady and the humble day laborer who bet on the same horse share this passion and are both equally suspicious of the **bookmaker**, who is almost certain to put their money, whatever amount, in his own pocket."

Coaches were also permitted into the central field and a few young people had climbed on top of one to get a better view of the races. They were cheering for

their favorite horses and seemed to know the names of the jockeys, too.

"People know the names of the best jockeys, the most famous stallions, or most promising colts, but don't ask them to name men in parliament, army generals, or, if I may, the best authors. And as for artists, they paint just about as many portraits of horses as they do of humans. Some have even specialized."

"Do you often come to the races, Mr. Dickens?" asked Alice.

"I do. I'm one of the many Londoners who have fallen under the spell of the hippodrome. I know a **lord**, an inveterate better, who in his sixty years says he has missed only two of the great Epson derbies: once in 1805 because he had the measles, and in 1815 because he was fighting **Napoleon** at Waterloo. And he's never forgiven Napoleon."

"But you don't bet, do you Mr. Dickens?" asked Alice in a rather disapproving tone.

Our guide laughed outright. "Thunder and lightning, my lass, a few **shillings** aren't going to send me to the poorhouse. Not even Charles Dickens can resist the thrill of the race."

Home Life

Alice and I had persuaded Mr. Dickens to show us what life was like for a family in London. He had brought us to a large, stone house and we were standing in front of a large window peering inside. "This isn't polite at all," said Mr. Dickens, "but I can't knock on their door and ask to bring you inside. Londoners are wary of things they don't recognize, and you are quite different looking."

"This is what a typical middle-class home looks like," said Mr. Dickens proudly. "Good solid furniture, a portrait of the young Queen Victoria over the mantle, carpets, and heavy curtains. Families usually dine together. Is that what your homes are like?"

"Not exactly," I answered. "But I'm not really interested in the furnishings, I'd rather know about the people."

"Respectability and decorum, my lad, that's what you see. Remember that the man is the head of the

family and master of the house. According to the recent women's magazines, the woman's greatest pride and joy is to subordinate her own needs to the privilege and duty of lovingly assisting him and being sweetly modest."

"There are an awful lot of children," observed Alice.

"The average English family has six," recited Dickens, sure of himself, "but there are some that have as many as twelve or more."

"And who takes care of them?" I asked. "My mother is always saying that Alice and I are more than she can handle."

"Children are taught from a young age that their first duty is to please their parents who, like God, must be loved and feared. And, of course, many middle-class families have servants to help."

The Queen's House

We crossed a park with ponds full of ducks and swans; gulls and pelicans flew overhead. Finally we came to Buckingham Palace. Mr. Dickens was bubbling over with enthusiasm.

"This is the royal palace, the official residence of Queen Victoria and her consort, Prince **Albert**. This is where the council of the crown meets, ambassadors are received, and the heads of foreign countries are entertained. But the royal family has other residences in London, like those in Windsor and Kensington, where they lead a more normal daily life."

"Have the kings and queens of England always lived here?" I asked.

"Oh, no," answered Mr. Dickens. "Buckingham Palace hasn't been a royal residence for very long. Originally, it belonged to the Duke of Buckingham and was bought by the crown in 1762. In about 1825 George IV, the present queen's uncle, decided that he wanted this as his new palace. Parlia-ment reluctantly set aside 200,000 **pounds** (£) to renovate it. Ten years later, when King George died, the palace was still not finished and £700,000 had already been spent."

"What happened then?" asked Alice.

"The new king, William IV, another of the queen's uncles, preferred living in Windsor. It was Victoria who moved the royal family here, barely a month after her coronation."

"So she moved in while work was still going on," I said.

"The Italian-style wing at the end of the courtyard hadn't yet been finished, but by 1847 it was all done. Most Londoners, including me, aren't quite used to it yet. See that flag flying? It means the queen is in residence. I had hoped you might catch a glimpse of her."

11

The Great Exhibition

"Where are we?" I asked Mr. Dickens. "Our London guidebook doesn't mention anything like this near Hyde Park. I would have remembered if it had."

"That's the advantage of having me as your guide. I can show you things that no longer exist. You are looking at the Great Exhibition, sponsored by Prince Albert."

"It looks huge," said Alice, "more like a fair."

"And that's what it is," said Dickens proudly, "a fair that celebrates science and progress, which glorify Great Britain. This is the first time ever that products and inventions from all over world have been brought together at one place. There have been 13,937 exhibitors and over six million visitors so far!"

"Wow, that's a lot of people. What's here to see? Where do we begin?" Alice and I were excited.

"Generally the public lines up to see the famous 103-karat Indian Kohinoor diamond, also called the 'Mountain of Light.' Military men prefer the great **Krupp** cannon or Colonel **Colt**'s pistol, which is in the American pavilion. There are locomotives, marine motors, and steampowered agricultural machines, all products of technological progress. Personally, I prefer the vertical printing press, which can print a thousand pages per hour. Even this building, known as the Crystal Palace, is part of the exhibition. It's a triumph of engineering and covers four times the area of St. Peter's in Rome! But what astounds Londoners most is that it only costs one shilling to come and see all these marvels."

THE CRYSTAL PALACE

The Crystal Palace was a premade glass-and-iron structure 1,851 feet (564 m) long and 408 feet (124 m) wide. There is approximately 1,000,000 square feet (304,800 m^2) of glass panes on an iron framework. It was designed and built by Joseph Paxton, a greenhouse architect, specifically for the 1851 Great Exhibition. After the exposition it was dismantled and rebuilt in London's Syndenham Hill district. The Crystal Palace was destroyed by fire in 1936.

An English Pub

"I don't know about you, but old Charles needs a break," said Dickens with a wink and a smile. We went into a large, dimly lit room that looked like an enormous cellar. Mr. Dickens elbowed his way through to a massive wood counter and shouted out his order as he went: "A pint of ale!"

When we finally caught up with him after pushing through a crowd of indifferent faces, he was happily drinking a mug of ale. "Nobody wanders around the streets of London, like we're doing, without coming into a place like this every so often," he said.

"Is it a bar? A place where you come to drink?" asked Alice.

"Much more, miss. This is a pub. The most English of institutions, if I may say so," said Dickens.

"And what's so special about this so-called institution?" Alice asked.

He took another drink and explained, "The pub is a public place where you come to quench your thirst, have a bite to eat, and chat with the other customers. You can also play dominoes or darts. All customers are equal here: laborers, shopkeepers, academics, and even lords. You can be sure there'll also be a police informer, quite unaware of the fact that the man next to him is a pickpocket."

I was still trying to pick out the people he had named when Mr. Dickens ushered us out of the pub and on to the next place.

In the Market

As we headed for Covent Garden Mr. Dickens continued, "Here in London you can buy fruit, vegetables, and fresh fish at every street corner. If you can't quickly spot the stall you're looking for, all you have to do is perk up your ears. You can hear the cries of the vendors as they try to attract customers."

He was right. The fruit and vegetable market of Covent Garden was a chaotic and crowded place where each vender was trying to outshout the next.

"You'd never know it," continued our guide, "but in the Middle Ages there was a convent garden here, where no one talked out loud but prayed to God all day. Now I'd say it's a good place to get a sampling of the human race, of the tremendous variety of human beings. Why, all you have to do is look at their faces and you've got a good cross-section of our English society."

As he said this he pointed to a maid loaded down with bags walking behind a well-dressed woman, a scissors sharpener, a match girl, a few day laborers, and a pair of ruffians being shooed away by tradesmen.

Wherever you went you ran the risk of stumbling over a ragamuffin who, as Mr. Dickens pointed out, might ask for charity or just filch the wallet of a careless passerby.

"Sir," said Alice, "a lot of the children here are working too!"

"Too many," answered our guide sadly, "and too long. They sometimes work ten hours a day. You might say the street is their home."

"Alice, would you like an apple?" I asked to distract her as I reached out and took her hand.

"No, thank you, Freddy. I don't think I want to stay here any longer. Can't we go somewhere else, Mr. Dickens?"

14

Trafalgar Square

"Here we are at last. This is Trafalgar Square," said Charles Dickens proudly, "another piece of London that's been completely renovated and is something everyone can enjoy. Trafalgar Square is the place to go if you're looking for someone. Sooner or later everybody passes by here."

We looked up at the large column that dominated the square, up to the very top with its statue. "Quite impressive, right?" said Dickens. "It hasn't been here long. The monument was erected in memory of Admiral **Horatio Nelson**, the man responsible for England's supremacy on the seas, and it was inaugurated by Queen Victoria in 1842."

"Way up there," I said, "the great admiral looks awfully small."

"Don't let yourself be fooled. That granite column is 185 feet high (56 m) including the statue of Nelson, which is 17 feet (5 m)." Dickens seemed sort of nervous and distracted, but he continued nonetheless.

"That building behind us, with the dome and Greek columns, was built in the same period. It's the home of the National Gallery and houses paintings by the most famous artists in the world, including Titian, Raphael, Rembrandt, and Rubens. Parliament sets aside a large amount every year to add to the collections."

Our guide was getting more jittery by the second and I realized that we had reached the end of our journey. So I said, "You've given us a lot of your time and have been a perfect guide, Mr. Dickens. I'm sure you have other things to do, though, and must get going."

"It's true, our tour ends here, where people meet and where they leave each other. Delighted to have made your acquaintances. I hope you enjoyed London," said Dickens.

"Good-bye, sir, and thank you," said Alice, "it was wonderful."

Dickens strode off, and then turned to wave just before he was swallowed up by the crowd in Trafalgar Square.

The Victorian Period

Victoria was born on May 24, 1819, at Kensington Palace in London, to Duke Edward of Kent, fourth son of King George III, and Princess Victoria Mary Louisa of Saxony (in Germany). Her father died a year after her birth. Up until her coronation, Victoria lived in Kensington under the unceasing watchfulness of her mother in an almost completely feminine atmosphere. During Victoria's childhood both her uncles served as king: first George IV, then William IV. Victoria's mother did not get along well with either sovereign. As a child, Victoria was kept in Kensington Palace and away from the court by her mother, even after Parliament recognized Victoria as heir apparent if King William, who was almost seventy, did not have a direct heir.

Victoria grew into a young woman, yet she still slept in her mother's bedroom, and had no place where she was allowed to sit or work by herself. She was charming, but not beautiful. She was petite with luminous blond hair, slightly protruding blue eyes, a pale complexion, and a youthful but composed posture. Victoria was only eighteen when the Archbishop of Canterbury, religious leader of England, and Lord Chamberlain rushed to Kensington at 4:30 AM on June 20, 1837, to announce that William IV had died during the night and that she was now queen of England. After hearing this, Victoria reportedly said to her mother, "I hope you will concede me the first thing I ask of you as queen: let me be alone for an hour."

The new queen had risen suddenly to the throne and was practically unknown to her subjects. In the early years of her reign, the assistance of her prime minister, William Lamb, viscount of Melbourne, was invaluable. He helped her acquire the sense of authority that permitted her to independently and confidently exercise the power and the functions with which she had been invested. Only one person had a real influence on the queen: her husband (and cousin) Albert of Saxe-Coburg-Gotha, whom she married in 1840 and loved with a tenderness and devotion that brought the queen the love and respect of her subjects. From Albert, Victoria learned to work methodically and with tenacity. He also taught her the virtues that made the court and the royal family a model of honorability and decorum. The royal couple had nine children.

In 1861, at the age of only forty-two, Prince Albert died of typhoid fever. With frightening swiftness Queen Victoria fell from a radiant serenity to a profound depression and became a recluse. Occasionally her subjects saw her pass in her coach: a robust matron dressed in mourning clothes with her favorite dachshund on her lap. The only politician to break through her isolation was her prime minister Benjamin Disraeli, who succeeded in gaining the affection and the esteem of the aging queen. Victoria made him Earl of Beaconsfield and he had Victoria, whom he called the fairy, proclaimed Empress of India.

In June 1887 Victoria celebrated the fiftieth year of her reign. In autumn of 1900 the queen collapsed; she died on January 22, 1901, ending her sixty-four-year reign. There were not many subjects who could remember a time when Victoria had not been queen.

Facing page: A photograph of Queen Victoria.

Below: The fog and smoke of harbors and railroads is an emblematic image of the Industrial Revolution in England.

Chronology

55–54 BCE – Julius Caesar commands the first Roman expeditions in Britannia.

43 CE – The armies of the Roman emperor Claudius establish the military station of Londinium, on the Thames. The fortified center would become the future City.

50 – A permanent bridge is erected in Londinium, turning it into an important trading center.

409–410 – Britannia rebels against Rome and puts an end to Roman rule.

ca. 450 – Jutes, Angles, and Saxons invade England and push the Britons toward Wales and Scotland.

864–899 – Beginning of the Danish conquest and reign of Alfred the Great.

ca. 1050 – Edward the Confessor, the last great king of the realm of Wessex, begins the reconstruction of Westminster.

1066 – **William the Conqueror** conquers England and is crowned king in Westminster. Construction of the Tower of London begins.

1191 – London obtains a municipal statute from Prince John Lackland (regent for his brother Richard the Lionheart, who is fighting in the Crusades).

1215 – King John signs the Magna Carta and confirms the right of London to elect its own mayor.

1348 – An outbreak of the plague kills half of the population of London.

1381 – Under the reign of Richard II, London is sacked by peasants in revolt; the archbishop of Canterbury is assassinated.

1455–1485 – The Wars of the Roses: the houses of Lancaster and York fight for the throne of England.

1534 – Henry VIII breaks with Rome and establishes the Church of England.

1558–1603 – Reign of Queen Elizabeth I: though England is isolated from the rest of Europe, it dominates the seas.

1584–1589 – Sir Walter Raleigh establishes the colony of Virginia, named after the virgin queen Elizabeth.

1588 – Sir Francis Drake defeats the Spanish Armada.

1590–1616 – William Shakespeare writes his plays, which define English theater.

1600 – The East India Company is established.

1607 – The Virginia Company establishes the Jamestown settlement.

1649 – Charles I is tried and beheaded. Parliament takes power and Oliver Cromwell becomes lord protector.

1665 – More than 100,000 die in an epidemic of the plague in London.

1666 – The Great Fire breaks out, destroying medieval London.

1670 – London expands westward.

1668 – The Glorious Revolution: Mary II and her husband William III, prince of Orange, accept the throne and the Declaration of Rights.

1700 – The population of London is 600,000.

1750 – London uses oil-burning street lamps.

1757 – The English take possession of India.

1763 – The Treaty of Paris ends the Seven Years' War and gives England control of Canada.

1764 – Public works begin in the Westminster district: the water and sewage systems are extended, the streets and squares are paved, and civic numbers are assigned to houses.

1773 – The Boston Tea Party. The American colonists protest in Boston against the English monopoly of the tea trade in America.

1776 – American Declaration of Independence.

1801 – The population of London is 900,000.

1803–1815 – Napoleonic Wars between England and France. Despite his attempts, Napoleon never succeeds in entering England.

1824 – The first railroad line is inaugurated.

1832 – The Reform Act changes conditions of franchise (Act of 1867 will expand voting privileges); a two-party system of Liberals and Conservatives is created.

1837–1901 – The Victorian Age.

1851 – The Great Exhibition is held in London, the largest city in the world with 2.4 million inhabitants.

1863 – The London subway (the Tube) starts running.

1876 – Queen Victoria is made empress of India.

1891 – Primary education becomes obligatory and free.

1901 – The population of London reaches 6.5 million.

1915 – London experiences the first air raid in its history, one year after the outbreak of World War I.

1921 – Independence and division of Ireland. The population of Greater London (City, suburbs, and outlying area) reaches 7.5 million inhabitants.

1931 – Creation of the Commonwealth.

1939 – The population of London is 8.7 million.

1940–1941 – German bombings (WWII) devastate London.

1944–1945 – London is attacked by the German V1 and V2 missiles.

1952 – Elisabeth II ascends to the throne.

1960–1980 – The port structures of London are closed and the city is de-industrialized.

1969 – Bloody fighting in Northern Ireland.

1971 – England joins the European Common Market.

1981 – The London Docklands Development Corporation (LDDL) launches a project for the complete conversion of the docklands, the largest European urban construction yard of the late twentieth century.

Glossary

Albert of Saxe-Coburg-Gotha (1818–1861), husband and first cousin of Queen Victoria of England. He profoundly influenced politics.

bookmaker (turf accountant), a person who receives and registers bets in horseracing.

British Museum, famous museum in London founded in 1753. It contains collections of Egyptian, Greek, Roman, medieval, and Asian antiquities.

Byron, George (1788–1824), English Romantic poet who became famous for his works with tragic and exotic settings, particularly *Childe Harold's Pilgrimage*; *The Corsair*; and *Don Juan*.

Colt, Samuel (1814–1862), U.S. firearms manufacturer and inventor of numerous types of pistols and rifles, which were named after him.

Debtors' prison, a prison for people who couldn't pay their taxes, rent, or debts. Imprisonment for debts was abolished during the nineteenth century.

Edward the Confessor (ca. 1002–1066), Saxon king who introduced Norman politicians and religious figures into the English court. When he died his successor, Harold, had to give in to the Norman forces of William the Conqueror.

Gothic, art style that flourished in Europe between the middle of the twelfth century and the end of the fifteenth century. The architecture is characterized by the use of the pointed arch, cross-vaulting with ribs, and buttresses. Gothic buildings have towers, spires, and pinnacles and are decorated with large stained-glass windows.

Handel, Georg Friedrich (1685–1759), prolific German composer: concerts for organ, sonatas, theater works. He composed 23 grandiose oratories, including the *Messiah*.

Henry III (1207–1272), son of John Lackland; he fought with barons over the Magna Carta and was forced to call the first parliament; renovated Westminster.

Industrial Revolution, the enormous technical transformation of industrial activities, which began in England in the eighteenth century and spread throughout Europe. The revolution is based machines that run on water and steam power.

keep, the most strongly fortified tower of a fortress, generally at the center, inside the walls.

Krupp, family of German steel magnates. In the nineteenth century the Krupp factories produced cannons and other war supplies.

lord, noble title to which the members of the Chamber of Peers have a right; also given to some public offices (the Lord Mayor of London).

Napoleon Bonaparte (1769–1821), French emperor in 1804. He fought against the European coalitions for power. England and Prussia finally defeated him at the Battle of Waterloo (1815).

Nelson, Horatio (1758–1805), the English admiral who fought Napoleon for control of the seas. He was victorious over the French fleet at Trafalgar, where he died.

pound (£, pound sterling), the basic monetary unit of the United Kingdom; one hundred pence are in one pound.

proletariat, the working class that possess neither the means of production nor a skill and are, as a result, forced to work in the factories and fields as wageworkers.

Scrooge, Ebeneezer, miser in Dickens's *A Christmas Carol* who is visited by the ghosts of Christmas past, present, and future.

Shakespeare, William (1564–1616), English poet and playwright. Among his masterpieces are *Romeo and Juliet*, *A Midsummer Night's Dream*, *Hamlet*, *Macbeth*, and the historical dramas *Richard II*, *Henry IV*, and *Henry V*.

shilling, a coin equivalent to 12 pence, or the twentieth part of a pound.

transept, the area in a cruciform church that separates the nave (where the pews are) and the sanctuary (where the altar is).

turf, a track or course for horse racing.

William the Conqueror (1028–1087), duke of Normandy. In 1066 he invaded England, defeated King Harold at the Battle of Hastings, and was crowned king, beginning the Anglo-Norman dynasty.

Index

Page numbers in **boldface** are illustrations, tables, and charts.